Other For Better or For Worse® Books

A For Better or For Worse® Collection

Things Are Looking Up...

by Lynn Johnston

Andrews and McMeel
A Universal Press Syndicate Company
Kansas City

ISBN: 0-8362-1892-2
Library of Congress Catalog Card Number: 92-72250

9

10

14

15

16

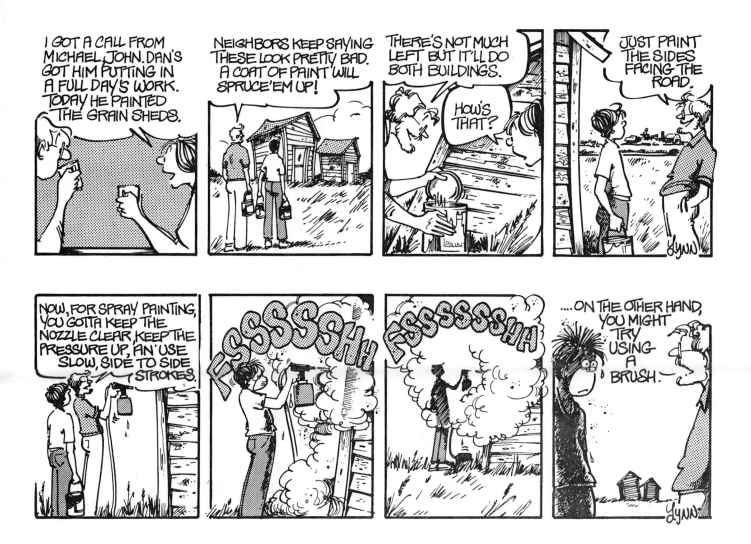

It took Dan, the hired man and me awhile to get Hermione into the half ton.

I thought she'd fight us all the way to the fair, but she soon settled down and enjoyed the ride.

Things got tense before showtime. My cousin, Laura, really wanted our sow to win.

The contest was a real who's who of porkdom. There was MUDONNA, HULK HOGGIN, SMELL GIBSON, MARLOIN BRANDO and even OINKLE SAM...

Hermione didn't win, unfortunately...

Phantom of the Slopera

1

... and consoled herself by eating her hat, her handbag and her corsage.

Lynn

It's different out here in the country, but I'm getting used to it, and you won't believe what I've learned.

Although there are no malls or fast food joints near here, everyone seems to know how to have a good time.

I'm working harder than I've ever worked in my whole life, and for some reason, it feels good!

Please don't show this letter to my parents...

I really hate it when they're right!

love, Michael.

Lynn

MY MOTHER ONCE TOLD ME THAT SOMEDAY, I'D BE PUT ON A PEDESTAL.

THAT A MAN WOULD BE SO DEVOTED TO ME, HE'D WORSHIP THE GROUND I WALKED ON... HE'D FOLLOW ME ABOUT...

THAT HE'D LOVE AND ADORE ME WITHOUT QUESTION — AND WHAT DID I GET?

.... A SHORT, HAIRY, OVERWEIGHT GUY, WITH BAD BREATH AND A POOR VOCABULARY.

Lynn

25

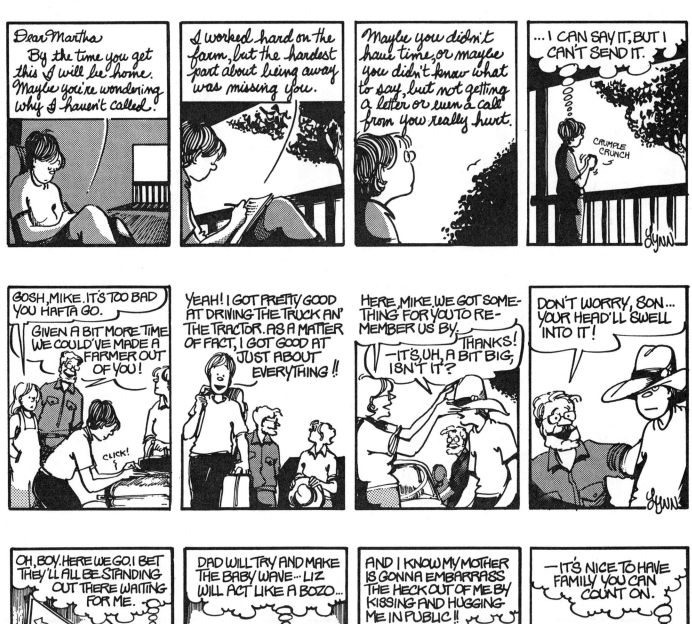

Panel 1: Dear Martha, By the time you get this I will be home. Maybe you're wondering why I haven't called.

Panel 2: I worked hard on the farm, but the hardest part about being away was missing you.

Panel 3: Maybe you didn't have time, or maybe you didn't know what to say, but not getting a letter or even a call from you really hurt.

Panel 4: ...I CAN SAY IT, BUT I CAN'T SEND IT. CRUMPLE CRUNCH

Panel 5: GOSH, MIKE. IT'S TOO BAD YOU HAFTA GO. GIVEN A BIT MORE TIME WE COULD'VE MADE A FARMER OUT OF YOU! CLICK!

Panel 6: YEAH! I GOT PRETTY GOOD AT DRIVING THE TRUCK AN' THE TRACTOR. AS A MATTER OF FACT, I GOT GOOD AT JUST ABOUT EVERYTHING!!

Panel 7: HERE, MIKE. WE GOT SOMETHING FOR YOU TO REMEMBER US BY. THANKS! —IT'S, UH, A BIT BIG, ISN'T IT?

Panel 8: DON'T WORRY, SON... YOUR HEAD'LL SWELL INTO IT!

Panel 9: OH, BOY. HERE WE GO. I BET THEY'LL ALL BE STANDING OUT THERE WAITING FOR ME.

Panel 10: DAD WILL TRY AND MAKE THE BABY WAVE... LIZ WILL ACT LIKE A BOZO... ARRIVALS

Panel 11: AND I KNOW MY MOTHER IS GONNA EMBARRASS THE HECK OUT OF ME BY KISSING AND HUGGING ME IN PUBLIC!! 204 WINNIPE

Panel 12: —IT'S NICE TO HAVE FAMILY YOU CAN COUNT ON.

26

34

37

43

49

ELIZBETH, IT'S BELOW ZERO OUTSIDE! PUT ON A HAT!

BUT, IT'LL WRECK MY HAIR!

AT LEAST PUT ON YOUR SKI PANTS!

AWW, MOM!!

FINE! STAND OUT THERE IN A FREEZING WIND IN TIGHTS AND A LIGHT JACKET.—I'M NOT THE ONE WHO'S GOING TO SUFFER!!

OK, EVERYONE. I GAVE YOU GOOD NOTES LAST WEEK, YOU'VE HAD TIME TO GO OVER THEM.—THIS MORNING, I HAVE A SHORT TEST...

A TEST? OH NO! AGGHH NO FAIR! YOU NEVER WARNED US!!

WE NEED ANOTHER DAY! CAN WE HAVE THIS CLASS TO STUDY? I WASN'T HERE LAST WEEK!!

GROANNNN

WHY DO I FEEL AS THOUGH I'M TEACHING DRAMA INSTEAD OF SCIENCE?!!

THE ANSWER TO NUMBER 17 IS MADAME CURIE!

THE INVENTOR OF THE MICROSCOPE WAS ANTONIE VAN LEEUWENHOEK!...

CELSIUS AND FAHRENHEIT REACH THE SAME POINT ON THE THERMOMETER AT MINUS 40 DEGREES.

...IT'S AMAZING HOW MUCH YOU CAN REMEMBER AFTER YOU'VE HANDED YOUR TEST PAPER IN!

66

69

73

HOW WAS YOUR HOLIDAY, LIZ?

AWESOME! — I GOT MY APPLIANCE OUT — AN' OUR BABY LEARNED TO CRAWL!

SHE'S INTO EVERYTHING, MISS EDWARDS. MOM'S PUT THESE FENCES IN THE DOORWAYS AN' AT THE STAIRS!

BOY, YOU DON'T KNOW WHAT IT'S LIKE BEIN' IN A PLACE WITH BARRICADES EVERYWHERE!

NOW, MANY WORDS IN SCIENTIFIC TERMINOLOGY COME FROM GREEK AND LATIN! FOR EXAMPLE, SOME COMMON PREFIXES THAT WE....

GROANN

Hyper Hypo

WHY DO WE HAFTA KNOW THIS STUFF? WHAT'S THE POINT? LIKE THE WORLD'S NOT GONNA COME TO AN END IF I DON'T KNOW THIS STUFF, IS IT?

NO.—

YOU'RE ABSOLUTELY RIGHT. THE WORLD WON'T COME TO AN END IF YOU DON'T HAVE AN EDUCATION, STANLEY....

...IT WILL SIMPLY PASS YOU BY.

MISS EDWARDS...IF EXERCISING MAKES MUSCLES GET BIGGER, WHY DOESN'T LEARNING STUFF MAKE YOUR HEAD GET BIGGER?

I MEAN, IF YOU THINK OF ALL THE THINGS YOU HAFTA KNOW — A PERSON'S HEAD SHOULD BE THE SIZE OF A BLIMP! ...BUT IT ISN'T.

SINCE EVERYBODY'S HEAD LOOKS SORT OF THE SAME...HOW CAN YOU TELL HOW SMART A PERSON IS?

...BY THE KINDS OF QUESTIONS THEY ASK.

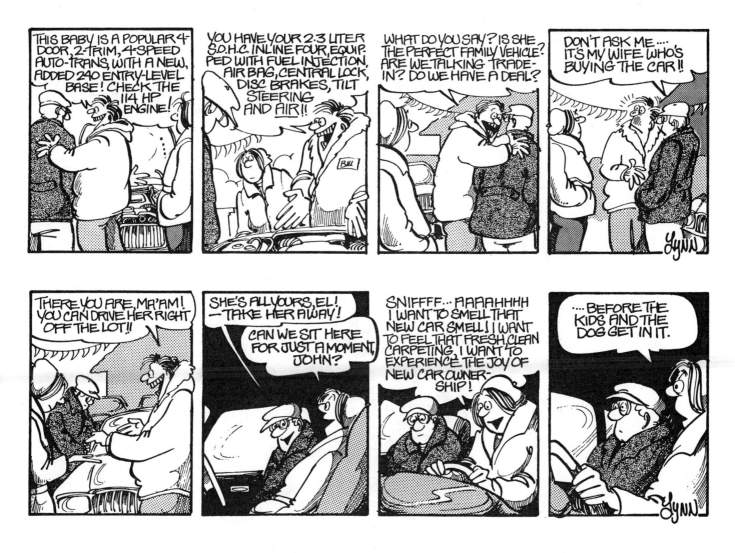

Panel 1: HEY, GORD! WHAT'D-JA DO?—FALL OUTA BED? / I WAS TAKING DOWN THE CHRISTMAS LIGHTS, AN' I FELL OFF THE PORCH.

Panel 2: GORDO! WHAT'S WITH THE BANDAGE? / I WAS TAKING DOWN CHRISTMAS LIGHTS, AN' I FELL OFF THE PORCH.

Panel 3: HEY, GORD—WHAT HAPPENED? / I WAS TAKING DOWN THE CHRISTMAS LIGHTS AN' I FELL OFF THE PORCH.

Panel 4: GORDON? / DON'T ASK.

Panel 5: GORDON, DID YOUR DAD... / IT'S THE TRUTH, MIKE. I WAS TAKING DOWN CHRISTMAS LIGHTS, AN' I FELL OFF THE PORCH.

Panel 6: I HIT MY CHEEK, AND I BROKE MY GLASSES. NOTHING SERIOUS, OK? / OK.

Panel 7: WHAT MAKES YOU THINK SOMETHING ELSE HAPPENED, MIKE?

Panel 8: WE WENT OVER TO HIS PLACE AT CHRISTMAS, BRIAN...THEY NEVER PUT UP ANY LIGHTS!!

Panel 9: I'D BET ANY MONEY THAT GORD'S DAD CUFFED HIM AROUND LAST NIGHT, BRI. HE JUST WON'T ADMIT IT. ...I DUNNO, MAN. HE OUGHTA REPORT THIS. HE OUGHTA SAY SOMETHING!!

Panel 10: IT'S PRETTY HARD, MIKE. YOU'RE TALKING ABOUT HIS DAD—NOT SOME STRANGER! ...GORD'S ALWAYS HAD HASSLES WITH HIS DAD.—HE'LL WORK IT OUT. .....IT'S BETTER NOT TO GET INVOLVED.

Panel 11: BUT, I **AM** INVOLVED, BRIAN!

Panel 12: .... HE'S MY FRIEND!!

YOU'RE RIGHT, DAWN.—I GUESS IT'S TIME TO WASH MY GYM STUFF.

WHAT'S THIS?

MY GYM CLOTHES.

THEY NEED WASHING.

WELL... WASH THEM!!

ME?!

ASK A STUPID QUESTION, YOU GET A STUPID LECTURE.

HEY, LIZARDBREATH!—IF YOU'RE DOIN'THE LAUNDRY, WOULDJA THROW IN A COUPLE 'A... HEY!—WHAT'S THIS?

OOOOOOHHH WOWW!! IS THIS YOURS?!

IT'S A TRAINING BRA, RIGHT? OR IS IT A SLEEP SHADE? WHAT'S IT FOR, SIS? WHAT'S IT FOR?

SNAP!!

95

Panel 1: DAD! / ELLY! ELIZABETH! / TAXIS LIMO

Panel 2: AND, BABY APRIL! LOOK AT YOU! YOU'RE SUCH A BIG GIRL NOW!!

Panel 3: YOUR MOTHER'S GOING TO BE SO HAPPY TO SEE YOU, DEAR. SHE HASN'T BEEN WELL FOR SO LONG. STILL... SHE GETS AROUND THE BEST SHE CAN. SHE NEVER COMPLAINS.

Panel 4: ...GRANDMAS ARE LIKE THAT.

Panel 5: HI, MOM! IT'S SO GOOD TO SEE YOU!!

Panel 6: SHE'S SO DIFFERENT. SHE'S SO FRAIL! I NEVER THOUGHT I'D SEE MY MOTHER LOOKING LIKE THIS! SHE WAS ALWAYS THE STRONG ONE!

Panel 7: ELLY! DON'T STAND THERE LIKE A LOST DUCK! — LET'S GET YOU ALL SETTLED IN HERE!!

Panel 8: THEN AGAIN... I GUESS SHE STILL IS!

Panel 9: I DIDN'T KNOW YOU WALKED WITH A CANE, GRANDMA.

Panel 10: WELL, I HAVE TO TAKE MEDICINE THAT MAKES ME A LITTLE DIZZY. SO... I CALL THIS MY THIRD LEG!

Panel 11: ALL KINDS OF STUFF HAPPENS WHEN YOU GET OLD, ELIZABETH. PEOPLE ARE LIKE CARS. THINGS WEAR OUT, THINGS GO WRONG, THINGS DON'T WORK...

Panel 12: AND SEE THESE SPOTS ON THE BACKS OF MY HANDS? / ....RUST!!

Row 1:

Panel 1: SHE'S A BEAUTIFUL BABY, DEAR—AND, BUSY! VERY BUSY!

Panel 2: SHE'S JUST STARTED WALKING, DAD.—SHE'S INTO EVERYTHING!

Panel 3: I THINK WE SHOULD PUT SOME OF THE BREAKABLE THINGS OUT OF REACH. YES!

Panel 4: ...AND WE'LL BEGIN WITH ME.

Row 2:

Panel 1: THIS PLACE WAS ALWAYS SPOTLESS! WHATCHA DOIN', MOM? WE'RE ON HOLIDAY!!

Panel 2: I'M CLEANING GRANDMA AND GRANDPA'S HOUSE, ELIZABETH. IT HASN'T BEEN DONE PROPERLY FOR AGES.

Panel 3: THIS HOUSE IS JUST TOO BIG FOR THE TWO OF THEM. STRANGE...

Panel 4: —EVERY TIME WE VISIT ... IT SEEMS SMALLER TO ME!!

Row 3:

Panel 1: MOM! I TOLD YOU I'D GET SUPPER ON! I'M FINE, DEAR.

Panel 2: I KNOW, BUT DAD SAYS YOU SOMETIMES FORGET THINGS. OH, I'M NOT THAT BAD!—HE WORRIES TOO MUCH.

Panel 3: TSK!—HE THINKS I'LL BURN THE HOUSE DOWN!

Panel 4: BY THE WAY...WHAT DID I DO WITH THE POT-HOLDER?

Panel 1: MOM!—IT'S GRANDPA ON THE PHONE! HE WANTS TO TALK TO YOU!!

Panel 2: WE'VE BEEN THINKING ABOUT MOVING TO A SMALLER HOUSE, DEAR... AND WE THINK IT'S A GOOD IDEA.

Panel 3: IT WOULD MEAN GOING THROUGH 40 YEARS OF STUFF, GETTING RID OF THINGS... BUT, IT HAS TO BE DONE SOMETIME. WONDERFUL, DAD! THAT'S GREAT NEWS!

Panel 4: ....THEY'RE GOING TO SELL OUR HOUSE!!

Panel 5: THAT'S RIGHT, PHIL. MOM AND DAD HAVE DECIDED TO SELL THE HOUSE. YES, I THINK IT'S A GOOD IDEA. YES... IT'S FOR THE BEST.

Panel 6: THEY'D LIKE US TO GO OUT THERE THIS SUMMER, GO THROUGH THE FURNITURE, THE PICTURES, ALL THE THINGS THEY WON'T BE NEEDING IN A SMALLER PLACE.

Panel 7: WELL, THAT'S THAT. WE'VE MADE UP OUR MINDS, HAVEN'T WE. I WONDER HOW MUCH THIS OLD HOUSE IS WORTH. I DON'T KNOW.....

Panel 8: —YOU CAN'T PUT A PRICE ON MEMORIES.

Panel 9: FLORENCE DILBUTT IS HERE, DR. PATTERSON. SHE'S A NEW PATIENT.

Panel 10: SHE SAYS SHE'S BEEN TO 4 DENTISTS, 2 DENTURISTS AND IS STILL HAVING TROUBLE WITH HER TEETH.

Panel 11: NO POINT IN LOOKIN' IN THERE. IF THEY WAS ANY GOOD, I'D BE WEARIN' 'EM.

Panel 12: TAKE YER PICK, DOC. NONE OF THESE DANG THINGS FITS WORTH A BEAN.

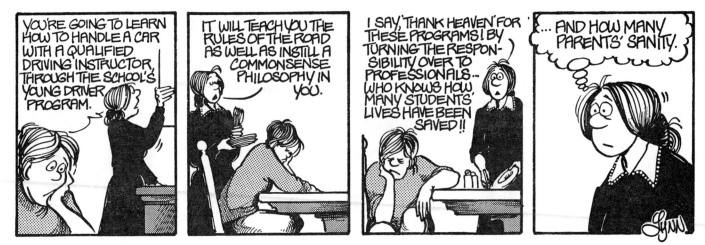

117

119

121

YOU'RE DOING WELL, MIKE, BUT YOU'RE STILL NOT CHECKING OVER YOUR SHOULDER BEFORE CHANGING LANES, YOU RELY TOO MUCH ON YOUR SIDE MIRRORS...

YOU DON'T CHECK THE REARVIEW MIRROR OFTEN ENOUGH, AND YOU DON'T ANTICIPATE THE TRAFFIC. ...YOU ALSO DRIVE TOO FAST.

THERE'S STILL SOME TROUBLE WITH PARALLEL PARKING, BUT WE'LL GO OVER ALL THESE THINGS TOMORROW. UH, OK. THANKS, MR. CAREY.

STUDENT DRIVER

PICKY, PICKY, PICKY.

WICKED! A 1990 MERCEDES BENZ 500 SL CONVERTIBLE! - AN' THERE'S A 1983 CAMARO Z28, A 1988 DODGE SHADOW, A HONDA CIVIC, AN' A PONTIAC SUNBIRD SE!

THERE'S A 1990 ISUZU IMPULSE XS, A '92 SUBARU LEGACY, AN' OLDSMOBILE CALAIS, A FORD ESCORT, A PLYMOUTH RELIANT, A GMC SIERRA SL, AN' A NISSAN SENTRA SPORTS COUPE!!

SHOW ME ANY CAR ON THE ROAD - I BET I CAN TELL YOU THE YEAR, THE MODEL, AN' THE MANUFACTURER! HI, MIKE!

OH, HI·· UH, UM·····

MARTHA!

OH, RIGHT. WE'VE ONLY BEEN GOING OUT TOGETHER FOR TWO YEARS AN' YOU FORGET MY NAME!

SORRY, MART·· I WAS CHECKING OUT CARS!

HONESTLY, MICHAEL, ALL YOU CAN THINK ABOUT IS CARS! FOR THE LAST COUPLE OF MONTHS, YOU'VE HARDLY TALKED ABOUT ANYTHING ELSE!

ALL YOU THINK ABOUT IS ONE THING! YOU ARE TOTALLY FOCUSED ON ONE THING!! - SOME OF US AT LEAST HAVE **OTHER** INTERESTS!!

...CUTE GUY! INBOUND - 2 O'CLOCK!

For Better or For Worse®
by Lynn Johnston

"The Novelty Wears Off"

"Insecure Days"

After the success of our first print, **Lynn Johnston** and **Stabur Graphics** are proud to announce two NEW limited edition prints of one of the most popular comic strips, For Better or For Worse! For years, Lynn has managed to bring to the comics that feeling of REAL life that we all can identify with.

"The Novelty Wears Off" relates, in a humorous way, the perception of most people that Christmas has become too commercial. **"Insecure Days"** looks at an emotion we have all felt from time to time.

- Each print is a six-color, fine art reproduction printed on 100% acid free, Saxony high-quality paper.
- Print size is 14 1/2" x 17 1/2" with an image size of 9" x 13".
- Provided with a Certificate of Authenticity.
- Signed and numbered by Lynn Johnston!

Each lithograph only $59.95!
(plus $8.00 shipping and handling charge)

To order:

For all orders, please provide your name, address, city, state, and zip with the following information:

1. The title(s) of the print
2. The quantity of each
3. The price each ($59.95)
4. The total price
5. Shipping and handling charge ($8.00 each)
6. The total cost
7. Michigan residents add 4% sales tax
8. U.S. funds only
9. Foreign orders add $5.00 to total shipping cost

(Credit card orders: indicate if AMEX, Diner's, MC, VISA, Discover– include your credit card number, expiration date, signature, and phone number.)

- Send a check or money order for the total cost or credit card order to:

   Stabur Corporation
   11904 Farmington Road
   Livonia MI 48150
   313/425-7930

- Or for faster service, use your VISA, MasterCard, American Express, Discover, or Diner's Club credit card and call toll-free 1-800-346-8940.